Fruit Salad

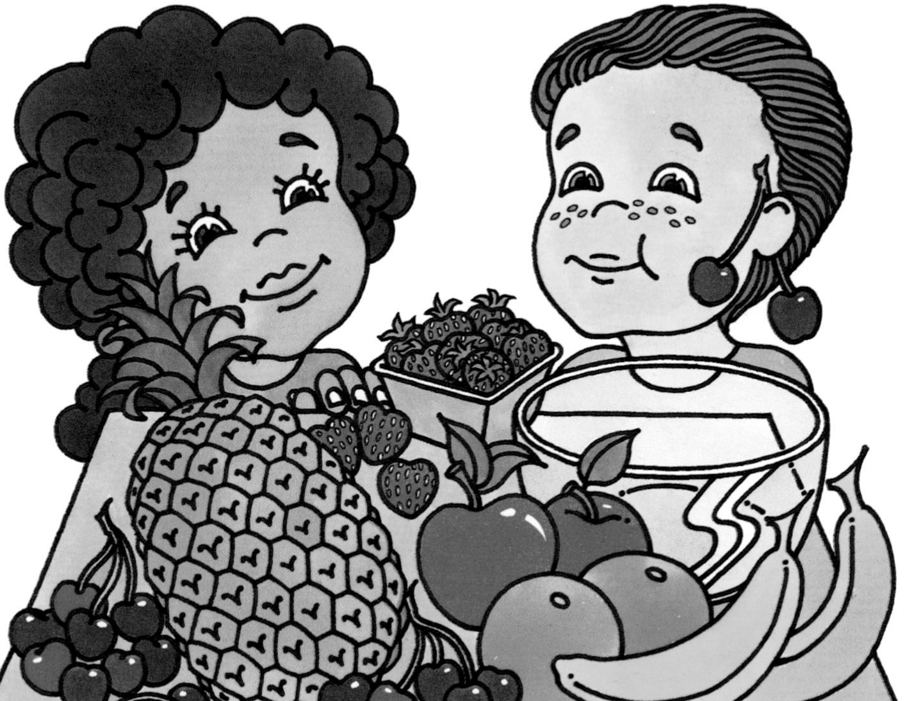

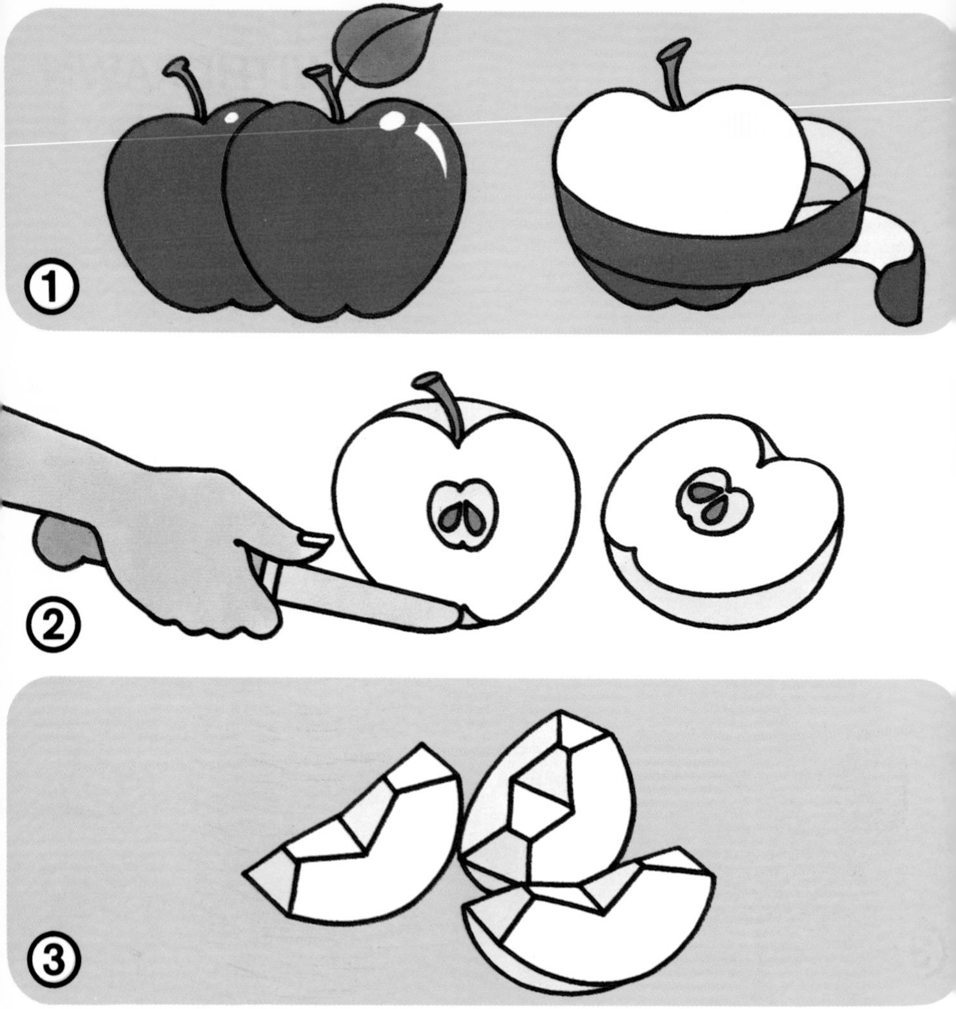

Some apples,

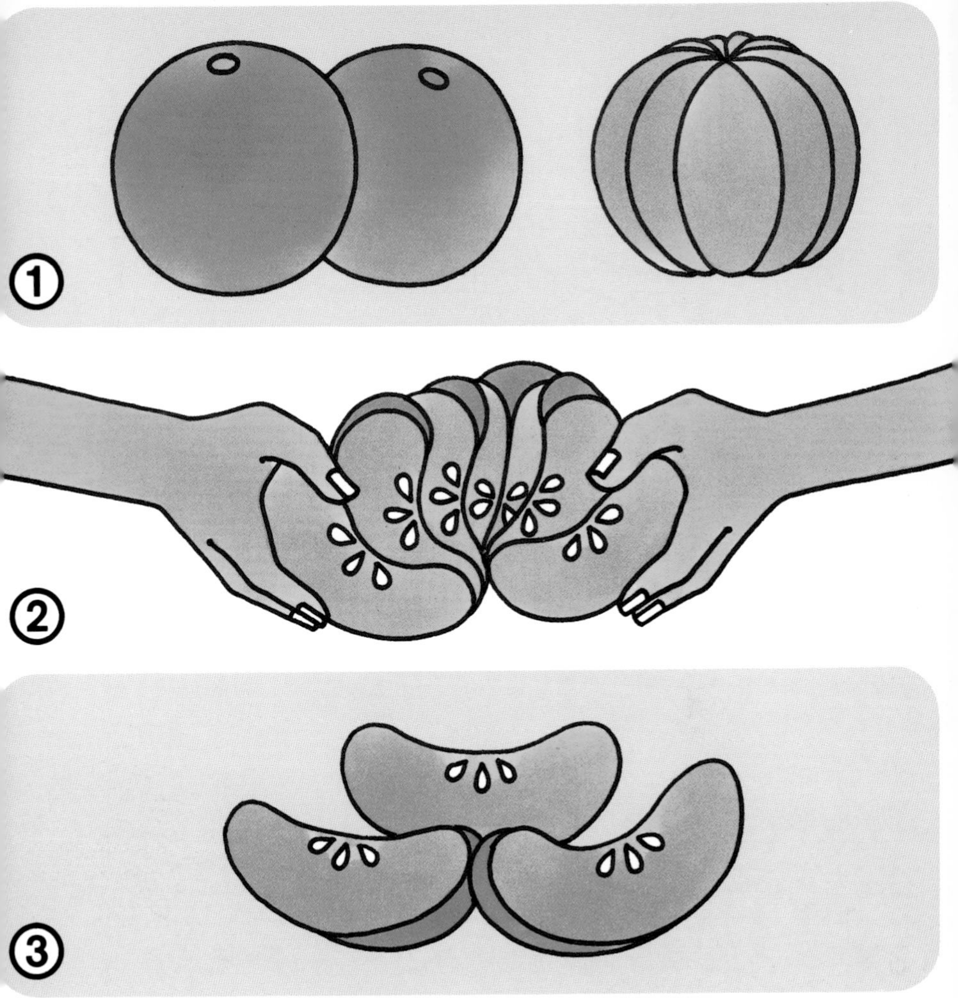

some oranges,

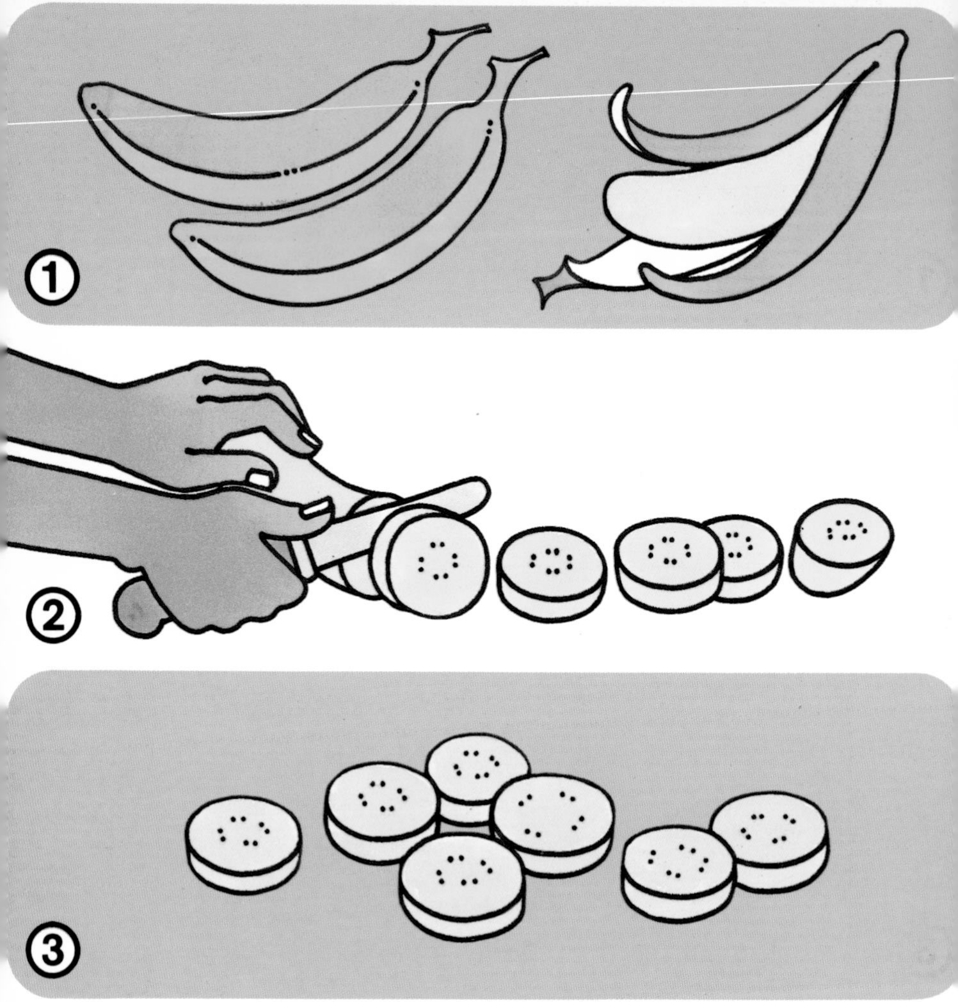

some bananas,

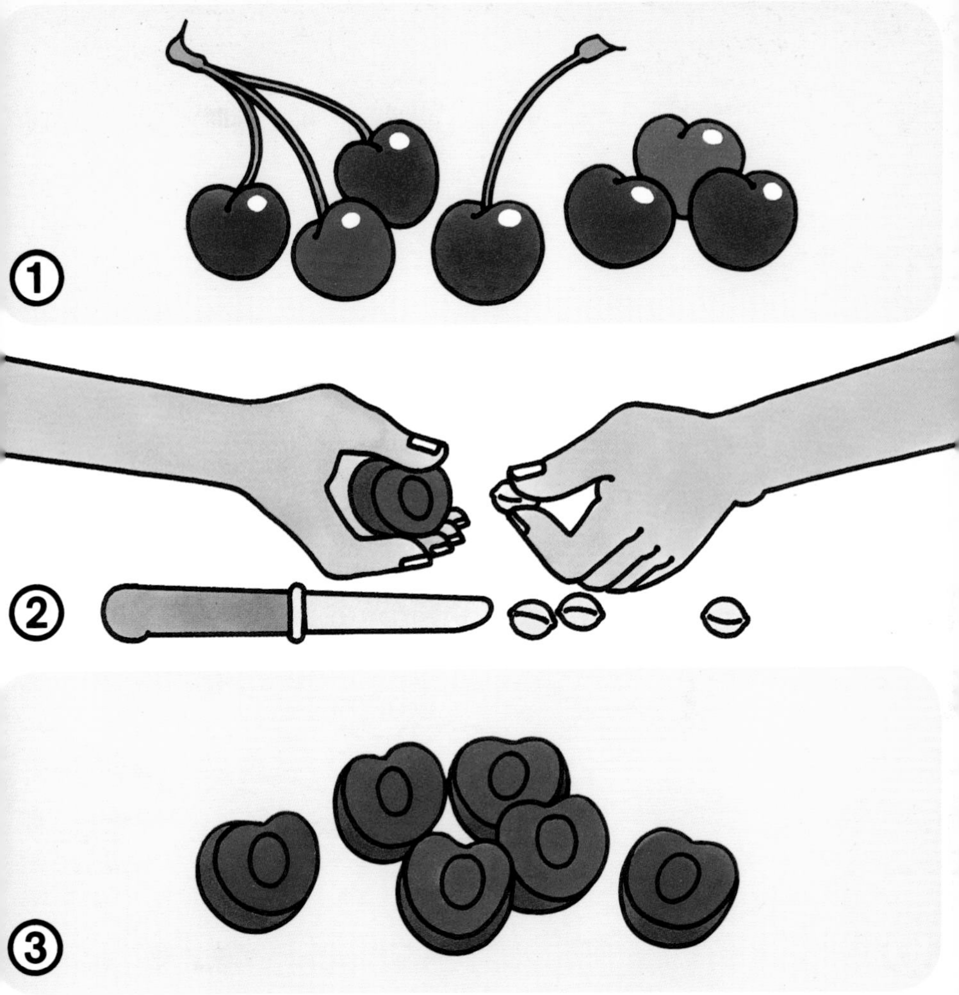

some cherries,

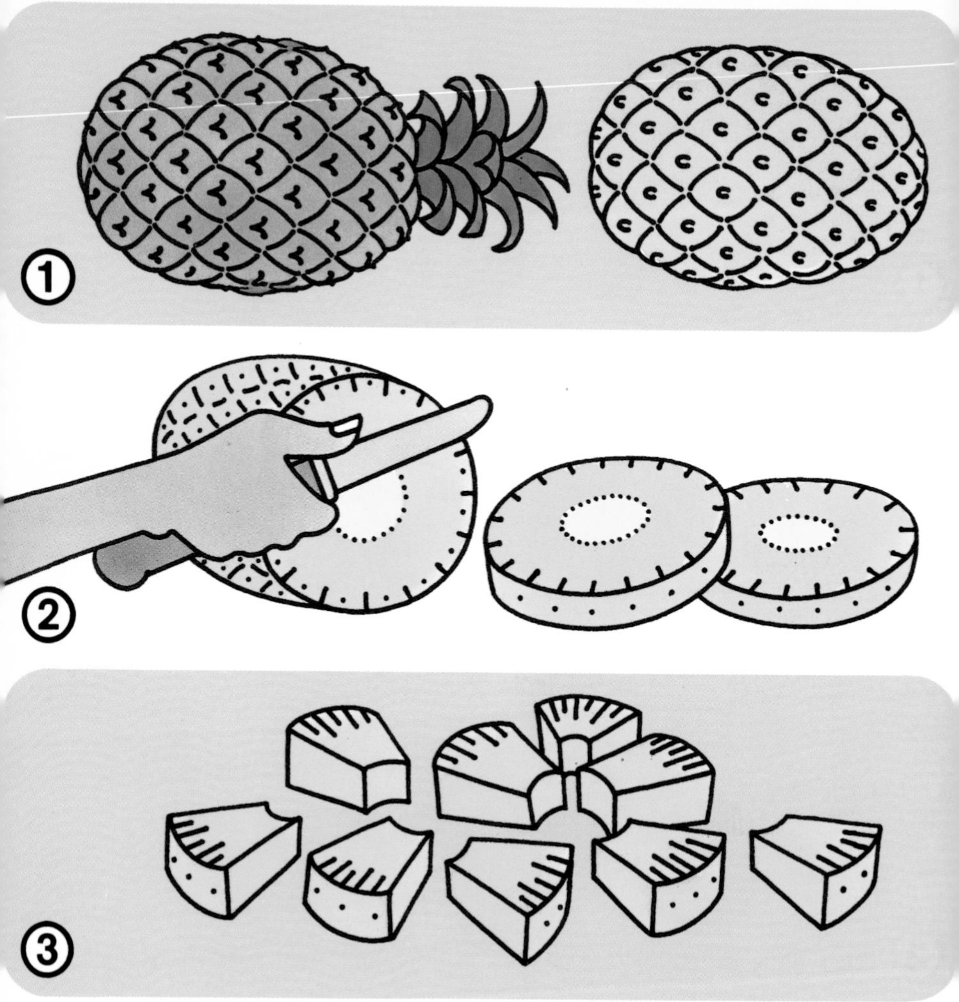

some pineapple,

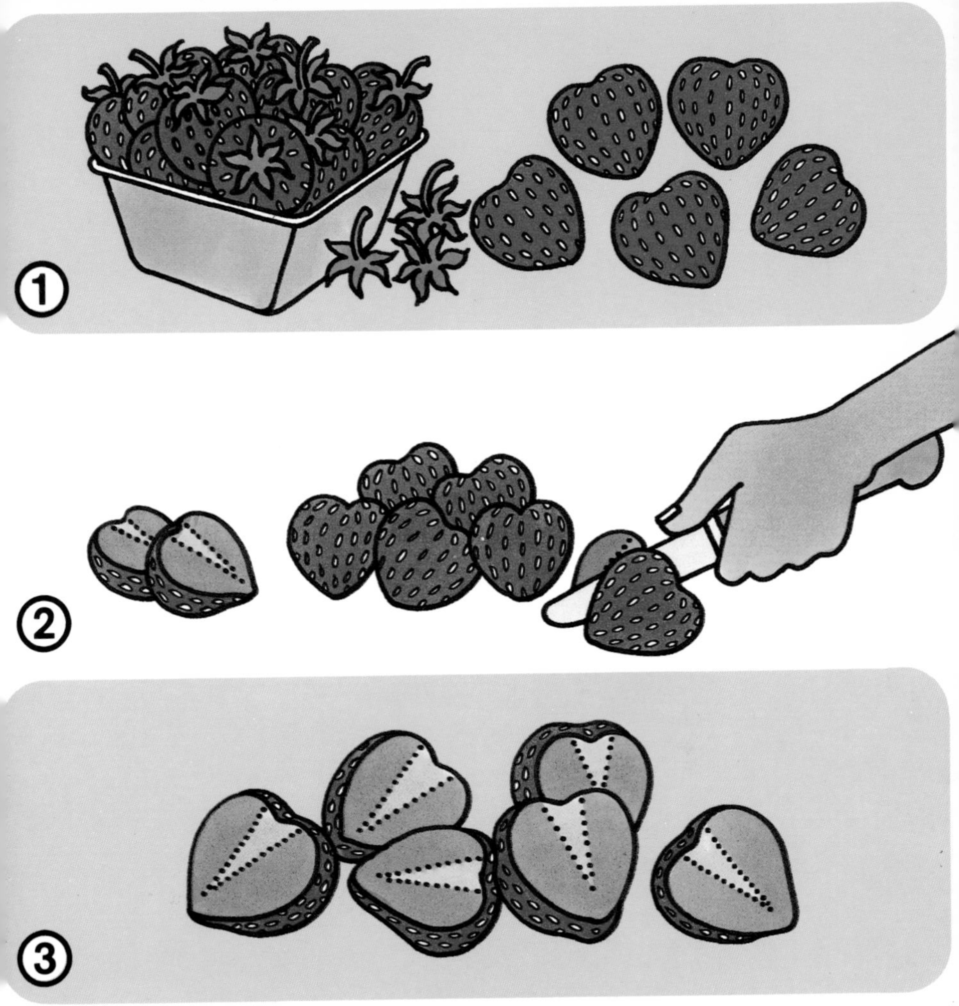

some strawberries...

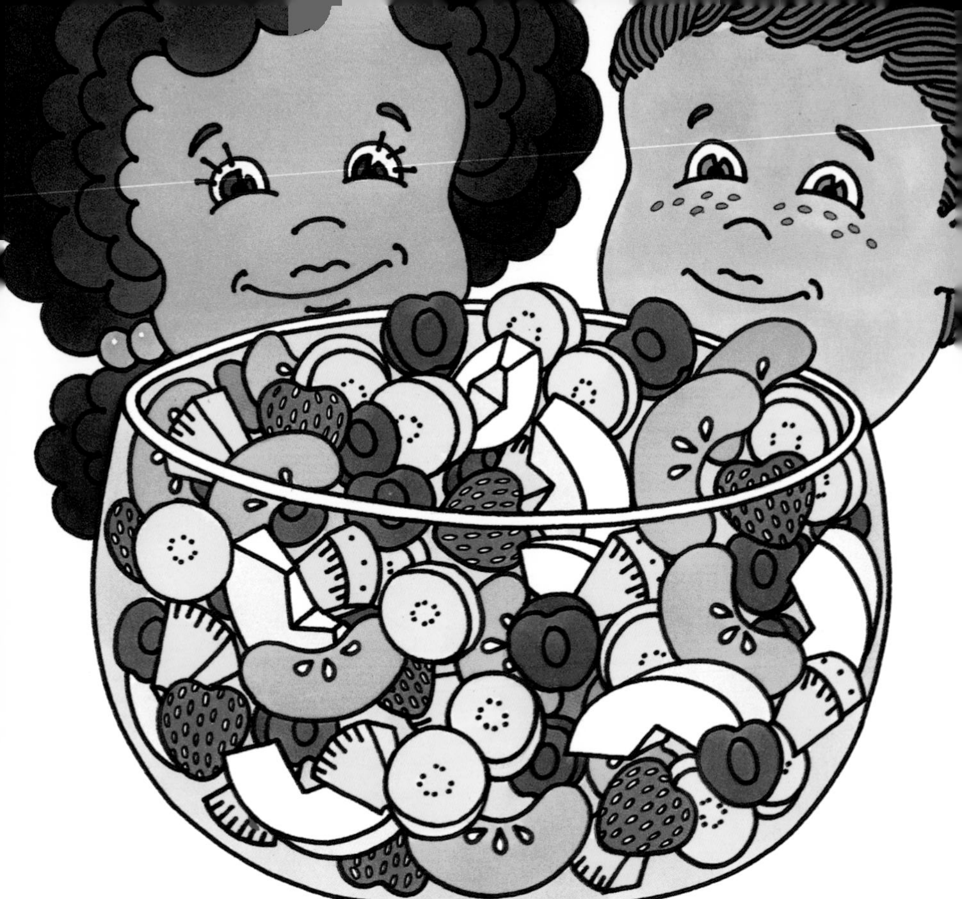

some fruit salad.